# GOLF
# THE SWING DOCTOR

March 1 2004.

To Keith
Best Wishes
Bill Branch

## BILL BRAMPTON

Golf professional at the European Club in county Wicklow, Bill Brampton has helped scores of golfers improve their game. He graduated from the famous Leslie King school of golf in Knightsbridge, London. Believing that the swing is the most important element in good golf, he chose to specialise in this aspect of the game. His technique breaks down the complexities of the swing into easily digested elements, ideal for practice sessions. Thus he earned the title 'Swing Doctor'. He has published many articles in *Today's Golfer* magazine and in newspapers in Britain and Ireland.

# Golf Lessons with The Swing Doctor

Seventy-two ways to help you win

Bill Brampton

THE O'BRIEN PRESS
DUBLIN

First published 1996 by The O'Brien Press Ltd.
20 Victoria Road, Rathgar, Dublin 6, Ireland.

British Library Cataloguing-in-publication Data:
A catalogue reference for this title is available
from the British Library

ISBN 0-86278-492-1

1 2 3 4 5 6 7 8 9 10
96 97 98 99 00 01 02 03 04 05

Layout, design: Frank Murphy
Cover photos: FRONT COVER, main photo
(Druid's Glen Golf Club, Co Wicklow), Bill Brampton;
small photos (top) Matthew Harris, bottom three courtesy
*Today's Golfer*; BACK COVER, author photo, Paul Harvey.
Cover separations: Lithoset Ltd.
Printing: Proost Ltd., Belgium

# Contents

Learning the correct golf swing is a conditioning process in which, by constant repetition, you perfect a sound action. In this respect, golf has a great deal in common with gymnastics, ballet and karate. In all of these activities, routine drills are carried out with a view to perfecting a specifically defined movement or technique. *Golf training should follow these same lines.*

As with other precision sports, as long as the golf swing movement remains a conscious action, you are still incomplete as a golfer. When the swing becomes subconscious and automatic you become a performer!

This cannot be achieved by gimmickry, by festooning the body with 'swing aids' or fitting it into mechanical swing-support contraptions in the vain hope of short-cutting the process of muscle memory learning. A computer read-out may tell you the speed and angle of the clubhead and so on, but it can in no way rectify your faults. You still need to acquire sound fundamentals and coaching from a skilled teacher and communicator. By studying the lessons in this book, I am confident that you will derive the knowledge and guidance towards acquiring a reliable, and enduring, golf swing.

As you work through this book you will find a method of play evolving – it is the 'no frills' classical golf swing as displayed by such golfing greats as Sam Snead, Jack Nicklaus, Tom Watson and Hale Irwin, whose swings have stood the test of time. They operate with the minimum of coaching to maintain their swing actions, thus leaving more mental and physical energy for the on-course job of winning championships!

To the educated eye, their balance and poise, and body reaction to arm swing, is clearly evident, and contributes greatly to their successes over long careers. So bear that in mind when you are considering your future in golf!

It is interesting to observe how the golf swing has evolved since the 'twenties. In those early days the emphasis was entirely on the importance of the hands – a loose, wristy swing was considered ideal. Then the emphasis in the 'thirties switched abruptly to the body, the hands being entirely passive. This theory still persists in golf today.

What is missing in these extremes is the vital role of the arms, which is the link between body action and the correct use of the hands! So what then is a rational and valid alternative to these extremes?

I believe that the hands create the swing, and control the club at all times, and that the role of the body is to move in a manner that assists and promotes the full free swing of

the hands and arms. Premature use of the body actually destroys the possibility of such a swing occurring, because it denies the arms the capacity to swing freely.

Therefore, if at the takeaway the hands control the club to the top of the backswing, then the hands will initiate the downswing – causing an immediate reaction in the feet and legs. This lower body activity establishes a backward 'resistance' as the hands and arms swing forward and through. THIS IS HOW POWER IS CREATED!

In other words, the body creates the conditions for a powerful and controlled use of the hands, and the agency for this is the feet and legs. This concept is the link between body action and the use of the hands!

If you want your swing to last for life, remember the golden rule: The body never propels (causes the movement of) the hands and arms!

*Bill Brampton – The Swing Doctor*

These popular Swing Doctor Golf Lessons by Bill Brampton are reproduced here more or less as they appeared in the newspapers. The success of these compact lessons is due to Bill Brampton's knack of making the contents interesting, positive, and sometimes thought-provoking, thus stimulating the desire to improve your golf. Above all they are highly readable.

Bill Brampton has brought good results and consistency to thousands of pupils through his inspirational teaching, based on

tried and tested sound fundamentals and delivered in a way that the student can understand. Bill sees no need for gimmicks, neither does he find the need to festoon his pupils with paraphernalia from novelty shops to get his points over! Rather he relies on demonstration, communication, and his skill as a teacher. You may use this book in many ways:

*1. As a reference for learning a complete, long-lasting method of play.*

*2. To resolve some of the golf swing problems that have often plagued your swing.*

*3. To open at random and discover interesting pointers towards improving your game.*

What are you trying to do in the golf swing? Not – as many try to do – blast the ball into eternity! First, you are trying to propel the ball from point A to point B (pic 1). This establishes the concept of a line from the ball to the target (pic 2).

Obviously, if the ball is to move along this intended line of flight, the clubface must be travelling squarely along that line at impact for as long as possible, both before and after impact. This applies equally, from driving to putting.

The ideal swing is a movement that causes the clubhead to swing into and along the intended line of flight, through the impact area, *and beyond*.

The longer the clubhead remains on the line to the target the more chance you will have of controlling the ball, particularly in the wind. You should keep these concepts in mind when practising your technique, and in that way you will form a good and positive approach to your game which can only lead to more consistency.

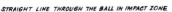

Players with this capacity for 'hitting the ball for a long time' are truly world-class. Two such players were five times Open Champion Peter Thomson, and Jack Nicklaus who won eighteen major titles.

STRAIGHT LINE THROUGH THE BALL IN IMPACT ZONE

The vast majority of golfers handicap themselves from the very outset with a poor address position. Either the body is too slouched or the legs too stiff or there is some distortion of the arms or head position. Yet when things go wrong with their swing, the last thing they consider is their posture at address!

The correct basic body position is vitally important. In fact it is the very foundation of your swing for two reasons: first it promotes and makes possible a free swing of the arms; and second it creates the conditions for the correct use of the feet and legs, which have a vital bearing on power and accuracy. So here is your address position review:

1. *Bend forward from the waist.*
2. *The back must be straight and the head held up.*
3. *The hips should be pushed back away from the ball.*
4. *The arms must be held clear of the chest.*
5. *The knees must be flexed.*

Check it out by using a full-length mirror. It must be correct in every detail if you are to gain full benefit.

Many golfers are unaware that the position of the arms at the address position can affect their entire swing action. Some players push their elbows inwards, with the upper arms tight against their chests (pic 1). They do so in the belief that it keeps their swing 'together'.

On the contrary, this is a dangerous habit because it restricts the free movement of the arms, which in turn causes too much 'body' in the movement. This is the prime cause of a golfer's lack of form in later life, because, as the limbs stiffen up, free movement is further inhibited leading to mis-hits and inconsistency.

You will certainly see a few young tour players adopting a tight-arm set-up, but they compensate by hours of body- and brain-wrecking practice, that eventually affects their ability to perform in the highest company.

So let your arms hang freely, and bow out slightly when holding the club (pic 2). This is a characteristic feature of players like Sam Snead, Hale Irwin and Jack Nicklaus, who win big tournaments in their forties and score impressively on the Seniors Tour.

Ensuring that the blade is square and at right angles to the line of flight is essential to accurate shot-making.

Many beginners become confused, and optically side-tracked by lining up the top, or trailing edge, rather than the leading, or bottom edge of the club. All too frequently the face of the club will be pointing to the left of target.

One of the most effective ways of avoiding this fault is to adopt a simple routine prior to addressing the ball:

Hold the club in front of you exactly as shown in picture 1 and observe the leading edge of the club. This should always be vertical. Now lower the club to the ground (pic 2), ensuring that you maintain the edge of the club at the same angle. The leading edge will now be at right angles to the line of flight. In this way your club face will always be pointing directly at the target.

Finally, while going through this drill ensure that all other parts of your posture and set-up are in place.

Many players have difficulty in deciding their distance from the ball. Naturally with woods you will be further away than you are with irons, but for all types of shot I recommend a drill which will place you at the correct distance each time, and automatically place the shaft at the right angle from the ground.

Take your grip and square the clubface to it. Now extend the arms and club straight out in front of you. As always, avoid any forcing or stiffening of the arms. Remember that the elbows should bow out slightly at address. Now, maintaining the angle thus formed between the shaft and the arms, ground the club behind the ball and move the feet into position.

Both the distance from the ball and the angle of the shaft will be correct. This drill holds good for all clubs.

In establishing the correct shaft angle, you will also resolve the question of the correct position of the hands at address. Holding the hands too low is a major cause of excessive wrist action – a vice to be avoided at all costs! A further benefit of this drill is that the hands are settled on the grip at an early stage, thus you will have more time to get the feel and balance of the club.

The most important rule when lining up your shots is to point the blade directly at the target. This may seem basic common sense, but many players either point their left shoulder at the target, or fail to take the trouble to ensure that the clubhead is actually making a straight line through the ball directly to the target (or the intended line of flight).

So your procedure should be to stand behind the ball and fix in your mind an accurate line to the target – perhaps spotting a blade of grass about six inches in front of the ball – which will then allow you to place your feet at right angles to that line.

It is also a good idea to have previously selected your club and formed your grip, so that you are already getting the feeling of the club in your fingers, thus saving time when taking your stance. This cuts out laborious and time-consuming address routines that do nothing but cause tension and delay – even before the stroke has been played!

The placement of the left thumb is so important that it deserves an individual lesson.

HAND TURNS TO RIGHT

The left thumb must favour the right side of the shaft and is placed in position by rotating the hand as shown in picture 1. The purpose of this is to to establish muscular unity between the fingers of the wrist and the forearm, to weld them, so to speak, into one controllable unit. The left hand and arm can now swing through the ball with firmness and authority, and in so doing will hold the blade square.

This will help eliminate the evil of rolling and collapsing the wrists through impact, which can only give a split-second glancing blow to the ball. Pursuance down that avenue leads to golfing oblivion – so avoid it!

To further check and consolidate this point of technique, grasp the left forearm with the right hand as in picture 2. Note that independent wrist rolling and breaking are eliminated. The hand and arm are firm, and will remain so throughout the stroke.

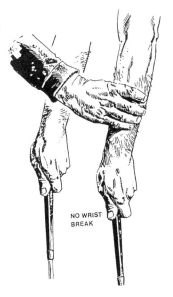

NO WRIST BREAK

It is an oft-stated fact that a good grip is essential for good and consistent golf. Sadly, beginners will frequently choose a 'comfortable' grip in the hope that somehow it will work for them. If only golf were as simple as that!

No. You must take care to choose a technically correct grip that will, when you get used to it, give you the best chance of reaching your potential. There are three options:

1. *The baseball, or ten-finger grip*
2. *The interlocking grip*
3. *The overlapping grip*

The 'baseball' is the least popular, because it can make one hand fight against the other, while the interlocking frequently allows the right hand to become a palm grip, rather than a sensitive finger grip. However, players with exceptionally small hands may find it has advantages – Jack Nicklaus did!

So we are left with the overlapping grip. This is where the little finger of the right hand hooks over, or rests on, the index finger of the left. Ninety-nine percent of tour pros make a good living by using the overlapping grip – so my advice is to follow their trend.

OVERLAP

INTERLOCK

BASEBALL

Watch any first-class tournament and the grip you will see most frequently displayed will be the overlapping. The reason for this is that it works so effectively in bringing in the low scores that win championships. So let's get down to its basic construction.

**Left**

The left hand (pic 1): make sure that the heel pad of your hand is seated securely on the top – not the end – of the grip, and that the pressure is mainly in the last three fingers. Above all, avoid the ham-handed palm grip of an axeman!

**Right**

Right hand (pic 2): bring this to the left hand with the palm facing directly to the target line.

Now join the hands (pic 3), ensuring that the little finger of your right hand overlaps the index finger of your left, and make sure that the tips of the middle two fingers fit snugly.

In picture 4 you will see the grip completed, the hands having now become one controllable unit. Finally, avoid the temptation to use undue pressure with the thumb and index finger of the right hand. Many unexpected swing problems can to traced to this fault!

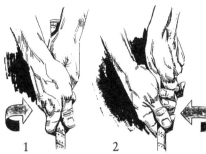

1    2

3

These technical terms often confuse the inexperienced golfer:

Weak Grip: This does not mean that the player is holding the club sloppily or loosely – although many players do! It means that either the left hand, the right hand or both have been turned too far to the left (pic 1). The product of a weak grip is a slice, or at the very least a lack of power.

Strong Grip: This is the opposite, ie, the hands have been turned too much to the right (pic 2). This in fact feels very strong and powerful, and becomes a favourite with some high-handicap players. The problem is that it will tend to make the ball hook to the left, and produce difficulties in playing long irons off the fairway.

The answer is to persevere with the correct grip (pic 3) and try to make it work for you. There is a well known adage that says: 'If you cannot work with the standard grip then there is something seriously wrong with your swing!'

If that is the case, you should seek professional help – or at the very least study my lessons, nos 7 and 8, on the grip.

It has been said that if a golfer has to use a bad grip then there is something wrong with his swing – and a chronically bad grip will cripple it. This is true.

Picture 1 shows by far the most 'popular' bad grip. The right thumb is positioned on top, pointing straight down the shaft. It is even more destructive when the thumb is positioned behind the grip, because it makes a natural wrist break impossible. Instead, wrists will fold 'shut', creating profound backswing problems, making the right hand too dominant, so that hitting behind the ball and vicious hooks occur regularly.

Picture 2 shows the 'trigger finger' of the right hand extending too far down the shaft. This is a legacy of the hickory shaft days, when players found it necessary to flick the head of the club square at impact, to counteract the excessive torque of the shaft. This is totally unnecessary with today's modern equipment, and should never be attempted.

Picture 3 shows what I term 'the axeman's grip'! The player has simply grasped the club in the palm of his right hand. It may feel strong but lacks the vital sensitivity of the fingers, and will keep you in the high-handicap category. The answer is to use the correct grip (pic 4), and stick to it. Given time, it will pay countless dividends.

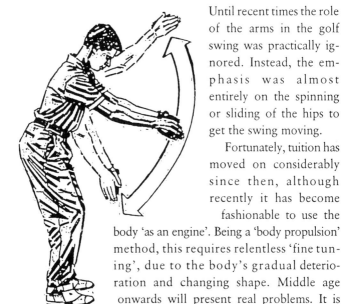

Until recent times the role of the arms in the golf swing was practically ignored. Instead, the emphasis was almost entirely on the spinning or sliding of the hips to get the swing moving.

Fortunately, tuition has moved on considerably since then, although recently it has become fashionable to use the body 'as an engine'. Being a 'body propulsion' method, this requires relentless 'fine tuning', due to the body's gradual deterioration and changing shape. Middle age onwards will present real problems. It is definitely not a swing for life!

By concentrating on the more logical and long-lasting system of training the body to respond to the swing of the arms, bolstered by a trained hand action and a square blade, you can expect effortless consistency through to your dotage!

So here is a special exercise to cultivate the feeling of a separate arm swing, so essential to all that follows in learning the classic, long-lasting golf swing:

Simply assume the correct address position (minus club) and swing your arms slowly up and down *while keeping your height constant*. Do it frequently, and do not underestimate the effectiveness of the exercise. The benefits will become apparent as you learn more about the golf swing from the lessons in this book.

It is surprising the number of players who consistently misalign the face of the club at address, either open (pic 1) or closed (pic 2). The latter is by far the commonest error, because the eyes will often focus on the top edge rather than the leading edge of the club. So focus your eyes on the leading edge of a square blade (pic 3) and always try to keep it that way. Lesson 4 will also help in this respect.

When you come to aligning your body, it is important that your feet, hips and shoulders are at right angles to the line of play, but it is paramount that the clubface is aimed along the exact line you want the ball to take – in the drawing this is from point A to point B. This set-up is known as a 'square stance'.

To check for, and if necessary correct, any

problem, go along to your nearest golf driving range where most mats have a right-angled line clearly marked, and place your clubhead beside it. Do this many times between shots so that your eyes get used to looking down at a square blade. This could be answer to your off-line shots!

Without doubt the best, easiest and quickest way of improving your golf is to review your address position. A minimum of ninety percent of golfers have serious faults in their posture at address. You will see many players in similar positions to those in my pictures 1 and 2. It is little wonder that things go wrong!

If this 'boring' part of golf technique was suddenly perfected by all players, it would have a dramatic effect on the standard of play!

So here is your check list for a good posture at address (pic 3):

1. *Bend forward from the waist, keeping your chest up and back straight* (positively no head down!).

2. *Keep your bottom pushed back and your arms held clear of your chest.*

3. *Finally, bend the knees.*

Unless these conditions are precisely in place, you do not stand a chance of making a good and effective golf swing.

Many players exaggerate their head position. The worst position of all is of course 'Head down'!

The ideal position for the head is central, or very slightly to the right. Players are often advised to incline the head well to the right and to sight the ball with the left eye only. These mannerisms are all very well for top players who have full control of their swing actions, but for the average player they invariably lead to error.

The head is a heavy part of the anatomy, and if its weight is thrown to one side it can seriously

affect the symmetry and balance of the swing. If therefore the head is placed too far to the right of the ball, it could easily shift to the left in the course of the downswing with disastrous results.

Experimenting with head positions can also lead to serious errors in the takeaway. In particular, the club can be dragged back too far on the 'inside'.

So, whenever weighing up conflicting swing advice, err on the side of simplicity. Any exaggeration of a particular aspect, say your set-up, could radically alter your whole swing, leading to confusion and muddle.

In the meantime, *do* look at the ball with both eyes. You've got two – so use 'em!

BALL
PLACEMENT

short irons
fairway woods
& long irons

DRIVER

Great care should be taken when positioning the ball. The rule is to avoid extremes.

At address you must first of all ensure that you are lined up correctly, that is with your feet, hips and shoulders on an imaginary line that is parallel to the intended line of flight.

When using your driver, address the ball opposite the left heel – never beyond that. As you move down through your fairway woods and then to your irons, the ball should be positioned progressively further back in the stance, until it reaches the halfway point. Never address the ball further back than this (except for very special recovery shots), as it will affect your arm-set, and consequently your backswing and the resulting shot.

Warning: some high-quality tournament professionals play every shot from the inside of the left heel. It works for them because of their highly advanced leg, arm and hand action. Many beginners have hampered their progress by copying this.

On the other hand, many successful pros play with graduated ball positioning, which is much safer for the amateur player, and recommended here!

SHORT
IRON

From a good set-up (pic 1), many weekend players will then ruin their chances of making a good swing by starting the club back with too much wrist action.

This comes from copying such players as Nick Faldo and Jack Nicklaus who 'waggle' their wrists during their pre-swing routine. It is very easy for the keen amateur to misinterpret this at the start of the backswing.

These preliminary 'waggles' are merely freeing-up movements or mannerisms, and should have nothing to do with how the club is ultimately taken back when the swing proper is commenced. In fact many professionals' mannerisms are misconstrued as points of technique to be copied at will, so don't confuse them!

The start of the correct backswing is a controlled movement, ensuring that the left arm, wrist and club are swung back as one unit (pic 2).

This is not done by either stiffening the left arm or locking the wrists. Instead the player should allow the left arm to swing back freely with a smooth, unhurried motion, eliminating all temptation to whip the club back quickly with the wrists.

Revising your takeaway technique, particularly the first twelve to eighteen inches, can, more than anything else, dramatically improve your game.

The takeaway is the first twelve inches that the clubhead moves back from the ball. A mistake here, and your whole swing is wrecked!

Very few golfers take sufficient care to ensure that the face of the club 'looks' at the ball as it comes back on a slight 'inside' curve. The wrists are either turned away (fanning), curled under (shut), taken back dead straight, or on a grossly exaggerated inside line. There are also other combinations and ideas which are bound to produce a variety of different backswings!

CLUB-FACE AT RIGHT ANGLES TO SWING ARC

Many gimmicks have been devised to try to ensure the correct takeaway path, from harnesses to metal frameworks, but like corsets, they are only effective when in place! Perhaps the most misleading advice is to try to lock the arms tightly onto the chest.

The way to ensure a consistent takeaway is to learn to swing the arms freely and without tension away from the ball. This cultivates muscle memory, which is the antipathy of gimmickry.

So study the drawing on this page and remember that during the takeaway, the clubface – the leading edge of the club – must be at right angles to the swing path at all times.

By observing this rule many faults, such as wrist rolling, can be avoided.

Unless the player has the club correctly positioned half way back, he has no chance of being correct when he reaches the top.

Very few weekend golfers attach great importance to this, but top pros do. Just watch them on the practice area at any championship – checking and double-checking. So you should take a leaf out of their books and study the illustration.

Note first of all that the shoulders have turned almost ninety degrees, and have not tilted. Then observe that the face of the club is vertical.

Practice swinging to this position, until you can get it right – every time. Avoid the two extremes of either rolling the face open or twisting it shut. Both of these will lead to problems later on in your swing, because, unless some correction is built into the downswing, inaccuracies at impact are bound to result.

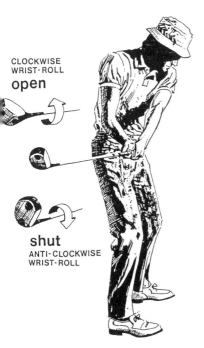

CLOCKWISE WRIST-ROLL
**open**

**shut**
ANTI-CLOCKWISE WRIST-ROLL

If you wish to have a consistent swing, it is imperative that you keep your action as simple as possible. This means keeping your blade square at the halfway stage, and consequently throughout the whole swing.

Avoid having to make compensations – at all costs!

The purpose of the backswing is to position the club ready for the downswing. It has nothing to do with power – that comes later.

The position at the top is critical, and must be precise. With irons it is slightly 'laid off'; with woods the shaft is horizontal and parallel to the intended line to the target. Many players make the mistake of trying to point the shaft of every club, including short irons, at the target. This leads to an overswing and erratic iron play.

**IRONS 'laid off'**

**WOODS swing completed**

When reaching the top of your backswing, always check that you have a full body turn, both with irons and woods. The sole difference is the amount of natural extra wrist break employed when using a wood. In this respect you should treat the swing with woods and irons as the same.

For example, no extra effort should be needed when swinging your driver. If the thought prevails that the wind-up is a source of power with this club, then a slice is the inevitable result!

You will notice that, if you are inconsistent with your irons, you will be worse with your woods. So get to work and practice to improve your irons!

A full shoulder turn is vital to correctly position the club at the top. But it is not enough merely to turn the shoulders. The right side of the body, from hip to shoulder, must be fully cleared to the rear to achieve the full turn you require (pic 1).

As the right hip goes back, it must not be allowed to rise. If it does the right leg will straighten – and you will not find any world-class players with a straight right leg when they swing.

When the turn is commenced, the left shoulder should not be allowed to dip. Instead, it must move across, maintaining a constant height from the ground (pic 2). In this way a full and free swing of the left hand and arm can be accomplished. This is the only way that you can achieve a natural, and effortlessly accurate, backswing position.

Finally, remember that the backswing is nothing to do with creating power – it is merely the means of positioning the club at the top.

The angle of the clubface (or blade) at the top is governed by the angle that the back of the left hand makes with the left forearm. At the top of the swing the left wrist should be slightly cupped. That is, the angle formed by the back of the left hand and the forearm should be about thirty degrees. This is ideal. This will place the clubface at the correct angle with the leading edge of the club vertical or at an angle of about thirty degrees to vertical – or somewhere between the two.

All other angles require compensating manipulation during the downswing, which will lead to inaccuracy and loss of power.

Nick Faldo sticks to the right principles – and who can argue with such an accomplished golfer? Nick, as most golfers know, changed his swing from the old, willowy, flailing action to a tighter, more controlled action.

This is my principal line in teaching, but I still see players, particularly young ones, ruining their prospects (and their backs!) with wristy actions. If you have ambition in the game you should follow Faldo, tighten up, and consolidate your blade angle at the top.

It is easier than you think to judge a good or a bad backswing!

My illustrations show the convex and the concave outline. The convex body shape is formed when the line down the back of the hip forms a convex curve, which gives the effect of the upper body leaning sightly away from the target. This is apparent in all good golfers, without exception.

Contrast this with the concave body shape, where the player's body leans towards the target. Another name for this fault is a 'reverse pivot'. It is frequently a product of the evil 'head down with stiff arms' syndrome. The trained eye can spot them a mile away!

CONVEX

CONCAVE

If you have any doubts, give yourself a mirror check as soon as possible. If you are convex, then you are working on the right lines. If it is concave, you have some work to do!

You may be able to do something straight away – by checking your address position and keeping your head up, instead of down! Alternatively, you will find a special exercise to help cure this problem in lesson 72.

Many self-taught and casual golfers, when attempting to turn on the backswing, actually tilt their left shoulder downwards, then aggravate the situation by straightening the right leg and lifting the right hip (pic 1). This combination is perhaps the most common major flaw among struggling golfers. From this bad position an infinite variety of mishits are possible.

So your first job is to set about removing the *dreaded dip* or *tilt*. This means learning to make a proper turn of both the shoulders and the hips by means of my special exercise (pic 2):

First, take a short iron from your bag, and push the handle into the ground with the shaft tight against your right foot. Hold it in place with your hand and then, as you make a swing with your left arm, draw your right hip and shoulder back to form a full turn. Never let the shaft of the club touch your knee – in this way stability and the centring of your movement is assured.

Once you can perform this movement with accuracy and ease, return to swinging your golf club, and try to incorporate the 'feel' of your exercise in it. It will be worth the time and effort!

Many swings are ruined by the straightening of the right leg, which then lifts the hip (pic 1), and in the worst cases causes a destructive dip of the left shoulder.

So it is worth checking that your right leg is flexed at address (pic 2), and it should remain so throughout the swing.

This inward flexing means that this knee should be pushed in slightly towards the ball, ensuring that the weight which the right foot has to bear will be mainly on the inside of that foot.

The reason for this is that the body turn takes place on a 'platform' set up by the right knee, above which the right hip is cleared to the rear (pic 3). The flexed right leg in fact supports the swing like a buttress, guarding against a sway to the right. This also ensures that a genuine turn takes place, rather than a rocking motion.

When practising, try wedging a golf ball under the outside of your golf shoe. This will help you to train the right knee to stay in place.

Is the downswing started by a rotation of the hips? For that to be true, it would infer that the hands are set in motion by the hips.

I know of no other sport in which this assertion is made. Swinging a baseball bat is almost identical to the golf action, but on a different plane. The baseball player clearly sets his feet and lower body to create 'resistance', then swings his hands and arms and releases the bat (against that resistance) with his hands and wrists, just as a golfer does.

No baseball coach would tell the player to spin his hips to get power, or for that matter to use his body 'as an engine', or to set up a chain reaction ending with the bat eventually coming round to meet the ball. That would be ludicrous! Yet these illogical theories still exist in golf today!

From this you will gather that the most logical way to start your downswing is with a downward movement of the arms (pic 1) in which the left arm takes a commanding role. The key technique – which requires training – is to allow the shoulders remain momentarily still and fully turned at the onset of the downswing. This sets up the correct

response (upward resistance – pic 2) in the legs and lower body.

Remember, it is the intention to exert power with the hands that causes body movement – not the other way round!

The exercise shown in my illustration is the foundation of the start of a good and consistent downswing. It develops the feeling of separation – or a genuine free left arm swing, independent of the shoulders. This ensures that the club 'drops into line' at the start of the downswing.

There is no way that this vital movement can be taught by strapping a student into harnesses and the like. No Open Champion to my knowledge has ever, when forming his swing, resorted to these measures. Neither should you!

*The exercise:*

From a poised position at the top, simply swing the arms down to the position shown while keeping the shoulders still. Then lift the club to the top again and repeat several times before letting it swing down into the back of the ball and through to a balanced, controlled finish.

The player in the illustration is using a driver for this purpose. I would recommend that the beginner or high-handicap player practice with a No 7 iron, and only progress to a wood at a much later stage in his development.

The overuse of the right hand and arm is very common and destroys a good clubline into the ball (pic 1).

Sooner or later the ambitious golfer, if he is to reach his potential, must learn to control the swing from the left side of his body. This does not mean ignoring the right side altogether; it means training your body to lead with the left side, and letting the right side stay passive until required.

One of the finest exercises for achieving this is to learn to swing a short iron accurately with the left arm only (pic 2). This is not done by aimlessly wafting the club backwards and forwards and trying to hit the ball vast distances!

It should be done with precision, by swinging the club to the top of your backswing and pausing. Then, while maintaining your balance and poise, swing the club slowly down again, tracing out your swing plane, and bringing the clubhead accurately to the back of the ball. This will give you the feel of left side control.

If at first you find the club too heavy, choke down the grip. With practice, even for a minute a day, this movement will become instinctive, and easy to perform. At this stage your whole game will have improved!

The prime reason why shots consistently veer off line is because the shoulders are 'open' at impact (pic 1), ie, pointing to the left of the target. Here you will also notice that the shoulders have turned ahead of the feet.

**WRONG open**

There are many reasons for this, but the main causes are when the player either uses his shoulders to 'get power' at the start of the downswing, or locks his arms tightly against his body throughout the swing.

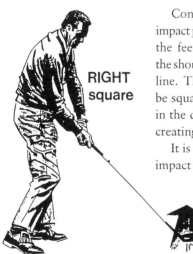

**RIGHT square**

Contrast this with the correct impact position (pic 2), where clearly the feet are actively working and the shoulders are square to the target line. Therefore the clubhead will be square at impact and travelling in the direction of the target, thus creating the desired straight shot.

It is interesting to note that the impact position is very similar to that of the address, with the exception that the legs have become active (in response to the free swing of the arms).

Throughout your training your thoughts should always be to think 'swing' and not 'hit'!

At impact the shoulders should be square, the shaft and clubhead vertically aligned, and the face of the club square (at a right angle) to the intended line of flight. If all of these features are in place, then the ball must go straight.

To help you achieve this there is no finer drill than the 'swing and stop' exercise. This is what you do:

Take a short iron – say a No 8 – and go through your normal swing action (pic 1), but stop the club at impact, ie, do not go through to the finish (pic 2).

Now check that you have vertical alignment* and that your shoulders and the clubface are square. Check also that your legs are working in coordination. If they are, you should have pressure on the inside of your right instep, with the heel slightly raised.

This exercise also has the benefit of standardising the release point and tells you whether or not the ball is coming off the middle of the clubface.

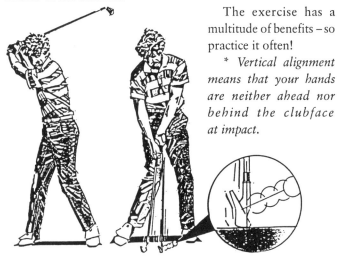

The exercise has a multitude of benefits – so practice it often!

* *Vertical alignment means that your hands are neither ahead nor behind the clubface at impact.*

In the downswing, the hands sense the release of the clubhead and the left heel responds immediately by returning to the ground.

This is the beginning of lateral shift. In other words, it starts from the feet up and is a response to the intention to deliver power with the hands, and to retain that power for the longest possible time.

In all sports involving the use of the hands, the feet and the body first set up a base, then the 'power' is applied with the hands. This is, in effect, setting up a backward resistance (away from the target) with the lower body, to allow the hands to swing powerfully into and through impact, and then to extend powerfully away from the body, up and into the follow-through.

Therefore, you must first set up the necessary 'resistance' in the lower body to generate maximum power with the hands.

It is a misconception to think that lateral shift starts the downswing – it is worth repeating that the lateral shift occurs as a response to the intention to deliver power with the hands. This concept is further explained in lessons 26 and 38.

**Exaggerated INSIDE takeaway = across line at top**

The swing plane is the imaginary line around which the club travels during the golf swing.

Imagine that your head is the centre of a wheel which is inclined at an angle. This angle varies with the height of the player – tall players like Nick Faldo will have a steeper (more upright) plane, whereas the diminutive Ian Woosnam's plane will be flatter (shallower).

From this you will gather that taking the club 'straight back' or sweeping it too much on the 'inside' can have dramatic effects on your own natural swing plane. The correct takeaway swings the club back quite automatically on a slight inward curve.

This is governed solely by the free swing of your arms, particularly the left. Therefore, no special effort should be required to place, or to consciously direct the club 'on plane', if it is done in the way suggested.

**STRAIGHT BACK = very steep plane**

**CORRECT takeaway = correct at top**

Notice in the illustrations the disastrous effects of 'straight back' and deliberate 'inside' paths! Avoid these exaggerations.

Misuse of the right hand and arm is extremely common in the downswing. It can cause both loss of line into the ball and loss of power. Both errors are highly undesirable.

In much of my instruction, I stress the role of the left hand and arm. This is because the left side must assume the commanding role in the downswing.

From the correct position at the top of the swing the left hand and arm take the club downwards into the ball. Meanwhile, both hands are contributing towards the control of the clubhead in the fingers and the wrists. However, the right arm and elbow are passive until the club descends to about hip height.

It is at this point (when good clubline through the ball

is assured) that the hands are in a position to safely release the clubhead powerfully into the ball (see illustration).

Most players over-employ their right hand and arm, so it is essential to train the left arm to lead in the golf swing. In this way the right hand and arm will have a chance to adopt their proper role, at the right time and at the right place.

That is why professionals practice hitting shots more with their left arm than their right.

The wrists must not collapse at or just after impact (pic 1) as it will cause weak, and often 'skied' shots. Instead you should train your wrists to remain firmly in control throughout this vital area.

This does not mean holding the club in a vice-like grip. Indeed quite the opposite is desirable. Holding the club tight simply builds up tension throughout the whole swing.

Your best course of action is to focus your mind on swinging your arms freely, eliminating wrist break at the start of the backswing. In this way you avoid hitting early from the top (see lessons 52 and 53), which forces the wrists to collapse through impact.

A good exercise is to swing the club and stop just past the impact area, checking that your wrists are still firm, and that the shaft is in line with your left forearm.

At first, this may be difficult because of excessive use of the shoulders, but by keeping your arms swinging freely and getting your foot action working (pic 2) the desired result will soon be achieved.

It is a fact that unless your movement through the ball is correct – that is, a square impact into and along the intended line of flight – the best backswing in the world will be of no avail! Your backswing is 'shaped' by what you intend to do at impact. Very few people indeed understand this concept!

Most players start the downswing by turning the shoulders first, while their feet remain static. They should do just the opposite. The following exercise helps you to achieve this, at the same time establishing a square blade through and beyond impact:

Pictures 1 & 2: Ground the club as if addressing the ball, then move the clubhead forward along the intended line of flight, at the same time ensuring that the right heel comes off the ground and the right knee folds in towards the left.

Picture 3: As the hands and arms swing the club into the finish, the blade must remain square and the body height unchanged.

Picture 4: Drop the club to waist height and check whether the blade is square. The swing is balanced on the point of the right toe.

If you can learn to perform this exercise to perfection your swing will quickly improve.

It is worth repeating that the purpose of the backswing is to correctly position the club at the top. It has nothing to do with creating power – that comes later!

In the ideal backswing the shoulders should be turned a full ninety degrees, and the left shoulder should stay 'up' as it comes around to meet the chin.

The right hip will be drawn back through forty-five degrees above the flexed right knee, with the left heel lifted slightly off the ground. The shaft of the driver should be horizontal or near horizontal, and parallel to the intended line of flight (pic 1).

There should no marked transfer of weight to the right leg, as this can lead to a sway. Rather, the right knee should be angled inwards (pic 2). This helps the leg to act as a bolster, or prop.

The body is now balanced, poised and ready for the downswing during which, to recap, there is an upward resistance in the legs, against which the left arm can swing, gaining the necessary leverage to create power – at the right time!

Such players as Greg Norman, John Daly and Ian Woosnam (illustrated) frequently amaze spectators with their spectacular long hitting. One reason why such professionals can do this is that they strengthen their hands. They also use the practice range every day, cultivating their hand actions.

The weekend golfer naturally wants to emulate these feats, but he fails because he rarely has that amount of time to work on his game. Consequently his hands are unable to cope with the strain of trying to hold a fast-swinging driver. He will subconsciously supplement his quest for power by using his shoulders. The ball inevitably slices off to the right, losing the very distance he was seeking!

Therefore, if you have limited time to practice, and need a few extra yards, with more accuracy, try these special exercises to

strengthen your hands:

*1. Squeeze a squash ball between each finger and thumb of both hands. Also crush it in your palms and rotate your wrists in both directions.*

*2. Suspend a brick or similar weight from a cord attached to a broomstick and wind it up and down. To make the exercise even more effective use your fingers only. This can be quite agonising, but it is worth it to get those extra yards into your drives.*

## Lesson 38 Counterforce = Power!

Newton stated that every action has an equal and opposite reaction. Therefore to exert force in one direction (in this case with the hands in the direction of the target) it is first necessary to set up a counterforce or resistance in the opposite direction (away from the target).

This is all that is happening with the lateral shift*. A backward resistance is being set up in the lower body to allow the hands to swing powerfully from the point of release through to the finish. So we can say that the strength of the resistance (counterforce) that is set up directly governs the amount of force you can generate with the hands. Hence:

*Little resistance=little force (1),*
*Great resistance=great force (2).*

Those who are thrilled by the phenomenal power hitting of big John Daly are witnessing the effects of counterforce. It is interesting that big John's idol is Jack Nicklaus who, in his prime, set up a massive 'resistance' that enabled him to develop corresponding power with his hands. This is perhaps why he asserts that his power 'comes from his legs'.

I would rather say that that his leg action, and the resistance that it provided, increased the power in his hands! Interesting isn't it? (* *See lesson 31*)

Many players, beginners and experienced alike, seem to think that the way you finish a swing has no bearing on the shot played. 'After all, the ball's gone!' they say. But working towards a balanced finish radically alters how your body responds as your clubhead approaches the ball on the downswing.

I agree that your backswing may be the root cause, and in obvious need of a major overhaul, but if you are looking for instant improvement, then attention to what is termed an 'on line' finish will start you on the road to improvement.

The player in picture 2 is a familiar sight on any golf course. The club has come abruptly off line as the ball is struck. This position allows no margin for error. Frequently the club will move off line before the ball is struck, with disastrous results and a cry of 'head up' from his partner!

The answer is to develop an 'on line' finish as in picture 1. Compare the angles of the body and the position of the club. Work to make this finish on every swing. This will widen your margin for error and help you to hit much straighter shots.

Lesson 35 offers further advice on this theme.

If the shaft of the club dips below the horizontal it is known as an overswing (pic 3). This is caused by the opening of the hands at the top of the swing. But the question is, why? Many would say that the answer is to grip the club tighter – but that is probably the problem in the first place!

This, combined with rigid arms, and pushing the clubhead back low in the takeaway, drops the left shoulder which in turn takes away the capacity of the left arm to swing (pic 1). If the right arm is above the left at the vital halfway stage this will further block the progress of the swing (pic 2). All that can move now are the wrists, and they break to keep the clubhead moving. In other words they break too early, and too much, literally forcing the hands to open at the top (pic 3).

From this you will gather that the hands do not simply open at the top due to a loose grip – they are forced open by an incorrect swing action.

The solution is to begin to overhaul

normal backswing

overswing

your swing, paying particular attention to the swing shape exercise in lesson 72. If you create a clear path for your left arm your wrists will have no reason to break early, therefore your loose-wristed overswing will gradually disappear.

Many years ago it was thought that it didn't matter whether a player developed a flat or upright swing. Gradually it was realised that the upright swing has many drawbacks.

**UPRIGHT.**
Club tends to go forward, **OVER HANDS** from top

For instance, it places the right hand and arm in a dominating position at the top of the swing. The right hand will thus tend to overpower the left in the downswing, leading to loss of clubline. Also, from an upright position, maintaining the club square and 'on line' through the ball places great strain on the back.

In other words, the upright swing tends to be destructive of clubline and leads to misuse of the body in the swing.

Any movement that causes discomfort or strain should be avoided, as it leads to fatigue and inconsistency. That is why some talented players with this type of swing will frequently fade over four tournament rounds, and fail to reach their potential.

Significantly, players from the past who were blessed with the flatter – and thus easier to maintain – action, are now making a large fortune on the Senior Tour in the States!

So the message should be loud and clear – if you want to stay swinging consistently throughout your golfing days, go for the flatter backswing shape.

**FLATTER.**
Club stays **BEHIND HANDS** on the way down

It is important to know the difference between 'closed' and 'open' stances.

If the right foot is drawn back from the target line (pic 1) the stance is said to be 'closed'. If the left foot is drawn back (pic 2) the stance is 'open'. The hips and shoulders must always be placed parallel to the intended line of flight.

Perhaps the only time you should consider using a closed stance is when you are using a driver off the tee. This encourages the clubhead to roll over through impact, thus making the ball fly slightly left. *High-handicap golfers should beware, as this may cause a smothered shot.*

The open stance is most widely used when playing a pitch shot or in bunker play – in other words when distance is not required. For the vast majority of shots a square stance is recommended, as this avoids complications in lining up shots.

It is very worthwhile to practice your alignment at driving ranges, because the mats will be set up squarely. Remember to choose a target to aim at, instead of trying to clear the perimeter fence! In that way your practice will be more productive.

There is no doubt in the minds of most teaching professionals that high-handicap golfers are obsessed with the desire to *hit* the ball – and to hit it as far as possible! This inevitably brings the shoulders into play (pic 1) and a slice is born!

Put two world-class golfers together on a practice tee – say Nick Faldo and John Daly – and which will have the biggest audience? Big-hitting Daly would win every time, but not necessarily on the course!

My message in this lesson is that big hitting, with reasonable accuracy, is the result of sound technique, built up through years of training, plus the commodity in short supply for most players – practice!

However, you can radically improve your scores, and consequently your enjoyment of the game, if you remove the word 'hit' from your vocabulary – totally! Then, in your limited practice periods, you should teach the hands and arms to *swing* the club (not *hit* the ball!) and build up distance gradually over a period of months, rather than minutes! In that way, 'clubline', so important for long, accurate striking, can be developed and maintained.

At the start of your downswing your predominant thought should be – think slow, think swing!

In lesson 54 I explain the problems of coming 'over the top', which is when the club loses its correct line on the downswing. This causes topping and hitting behind the ball, so it is essential to try to eliminate this fault.

One of the simplest, yet effective, methods is to swing with the left arm tracing out the path that the shaft should take on the downswing. Here's how:

Take your normal address position. Then swing your left arm (only) to the top of the backswing, ensuring that you have fully cleared your hips and shoulders. Now swing

this arm down across your chest, directing your hand towards the ball while keeping your shoulders still, as in picture 1.

Repeat the movement several times and incorporate it into your practice routine whenever you feel the need.

If you now refer to picture 2 you can see how this exercise will train your club to follow the correct downswing path.

This easy exercise has many benefits – so don't ignore it!

Correct foot action has always been the foundation of a good golf swing.

Many high-handicap golfers simply anchor their feet to the ground and believe that the safest thing to do is to leave them there! This has the unfortunate effect of allowing the shoulders to take priority on the downswing, leading to many wayward shots, particularly the dreaded slice.

At address position, the feet should be planted firmly on the ground with the weight neither on the toes nor the heels. On the

backswing the weight should favour the inside of the right foot, and the left heel should be raised slightly.

At the start of the downswing the feet become extremely active. The right knee kicks in towards the target and the weight shifts rapidly to the outside of the left foot, causing it to keel over. On the finish the swing is held in balance by the point of the right toe. This is evident in all first-class players, and is a point to remember when tempted to stay flat-footed!

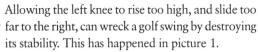

Allowing the left knee to rise too high, and slide too far to the right, can wreck a golf swing by destroying its stability. This has happened in picture 1.

In picture 2 the player is prematurely rolling his left foot inwards, which encourages the dropping of the left shoulder and the straightening of the right leg. This will produce a 'rocking' movement rather than a proper turn.

Compare the position with picture 3, where the player's heel has risen just a fraction, and his knee is pointing slightly behind the ball. You will notice that there is no hint of a sway.

So how exactly should the left foot be used?

Study picture 4, noting that the heel alone has risen slightly. The rest of the foot is in contact with the ground. As the heel rises, the foot breaks at the toe joints. This concentrates weight mainly on the big toe, putting pressure on the inside of that foot. *This is not the same as rolling the foot inwards!*

The left heel begins to rise as the club nears the top of the backswing, and not before. Premature rolling or lifting never happens in world-class swings, so learn to incorporate the correct movement into your action!

When top players complete their swings, the vast majority will lower the club to their waist and check the angle of the blade (pic 1).

The average club golfer will dismiss this part of his swing as a irrelevant waste of time. He does not realise that checking the blade helps to consolidate and maintain a consistent action. The blade check enables you to identify how your clubhead reacted through the ball at impact, thus:

If it was open, you've probably pushed or sliced the ball.

If closed, then no doubt you have hooked the ball to the left.

With a square blade – which is what you are seeking – the ball should have flown straight. If if didn't, then it will tell you that the fault lies elsewhere in your swing.

This information allows you to more readily self-diagnose your swing faults.

On the tournament practice area you will always see the top pros finishing in the way described. Do they think it is irrelevant? Of course not! So begin to form this good habit next time you practice.

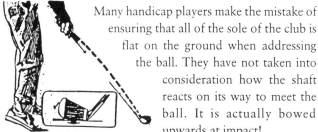

Many handicap players make the mistake of ensuring that all of the sole of the club is flat on the ground when addressing the ball. They have not taken into consideration how the shaft reacts on its way to meet the ball. It is actually bowed upwards at impact!

As Michael Caine might say: 'Not a lotta people know that!'

You can see this phenomenon quite clearly in the picture of the author striking the ball. Notice how the shaft has curved. This is more clearly shown in the small picture inset.

From this it is clear why qualified golf pros should always be consulted when you are purchasing a new set of clubs. The 'lie' of the club is crucial if you are not average height. You may be wooed by the price tag of some clubs that take your fancy, only to find out later that the lie of the club is totally unsuitable for you.

So check your position at the ball to make sure that the toe of the club is slightly off the ground. This will counteract the action of the bend of the shaft.

If you make the mistake of keeping the sole flat, it will result in the toe end of the club hitting the ground first, spinning the blade open and causing a slice. Maybe that's your problem – so check it out now!

If you want shots of uniform length and accuracy, you must standardise the 'release point' in your swing.

In picture 1 the angle formed by the shaft of the club and the arm at the top is preserved in a correct downswing, until the hands descend to about waist height. This angle has been maintained simply because the hands and wrists have not yet 'released' the clubhead.

Thus it is wrong to think of 'delaying the hit', 'hitting late' or 'holding back the clubhead with the hands'. All of these concepts tend to 'put the brakes on' the smooth and progressive development of power, and are inclined to destroy timing, rather than assist it.

The correct release calls for a gradual yet progressive build-up of power, like a car accelerating smoothly (pic 2). Then the hands and wrists have time to sense the correct instant of the release. Thus the angle is automatically preserved – there is no conscious 'holding back'. Power is gradually created. So try not to impede this process with bad concepts!

Training will enable you to identify the release point in your swing and, once you have it fixed, to retain it. Lessons 27 and 30 will help in this respect.

The illustration (pic 1) shows what is meant by 'across the line' at the top. Clearly the shaft is pointing well to the right of the target instead of directly at it, as in picture 2.

'Across the line' is caused mainly by the club being dragged too far on the 'inside' during the takeaway, combined with a dip of the left shoulder. This tilts the body in such a way as to make 'crossed line' a virtual certainty.

The immediate remedy is to review your technique on the takeaway. Take the club back straighter and with more freedom of movement in the arms, and hold your head and left shoulder higher as you swing. Don't forget to keep your right leg flexed!

This will give you a better chance of being correct at the top (pic 2) because it will place the club in the desired plane. The left hand and arm then reverse the direction into the downswing, so that the club will simply swing down 'behind the hands' and remain in the same plane, ensuring a correct clubline down into the ball.

A better impact will then result, directing the ball along the intended line of flight to the target.

Many golfers start down from the top by turning their shoulders. This is brought about by many factors, such as failure to use the feet in the downswing, an incorrect backswing, a desire to 'hit' rather than swing or the neglect of the left hand and arm in your action.

However, the commonest cause among experienced golfers is starting the downswing with the hips. The effect of this is to take the club off the correct downswing path, looping it forward on the 'outside' line. The result is the 'hackers' well-known slice.

If you are plagued with these problems you will now realise that your swing is in urgent need of attention! One thing is clear, neither you nor your partner – who perhaps likes to give advice – can put you right. Neither is it the old chestnut of 'head up'!

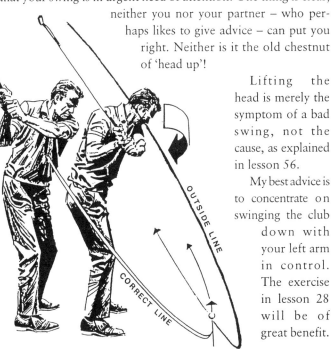

OUTSIDE LINE

CORRECT LINE

Lifting the head is merely the symptom of a bad swing, not the cause, as explained in lesson 56.

My best advice is to concentrate on swinging the club down with your left arm in control. The exercise in lesson 28 will be of great benefit.

When you see such long drivers as Ian Woosnam or John Daly crash the ball over 250 yards down the fairway you may well wonder where the power comes from. One thing is certain – it does not come from trying to *hit* the ball!

The average player when attempting to do this will usually hit early (pic 1). In other words, he will release the clubhead early. The secret with all long hitters is the correct release of the club – at the right time! (pic 2).

This was, at one time, termed the 'late hit' – a misleading description that often led players to consciously hold the club back in an attempt to whip the clubhead through at the last minute, instead of letting it swing. You should aim for a natural and progressive build-up of power (pic 2). This can only be learned by practice. Lessons 37 and 38 will help you to understand how power is developed and generated.

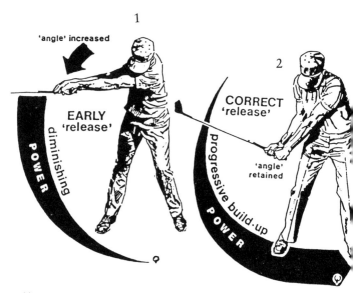

One of the most common downswing faults is 'throwing out' or 'fishing' from the top of the swing.

This is a very early release of power and is caused primarily by overanxiety to hit the ball. It is also associated with a very fast swing. By releasing the power early, the clubhead overtakes the hands before impact, resulting in a very weak shot.

It is quite possible to 'throw out', yet maintain a good line to the ball. However, since your power has been released early, it is almost certain that your point of release will vary with each swing. Thus shots with the same club will differ in length as the point of release varies, making club selection a lottery. Worst of all, it causes hitting the ground behind the ball.

To correct this fault, keep the clubhead 'behind the hands' on the way down and allow the left arm to make the initial movement at the start of the downswing. Lessons 26, 27 and 28 will help in this respect.

Finally, train your hands to release the clubhead when they reach about hip height.

ARLY RELEASE=
lub·head PAST
ands at impact

The purpose of this lesson is to define 'over the top'. It is a phrase used to describe a downswing fault which can afflict both amateurs and professionals.

Swinging 'over the top' happens when the clubhead is forced out of plane – compare the correct line, picture 1, with picture 2 which is 'over the top', and you will see clearly what has happened. The club has obviously taken the wrong route to the ball!

This is the cause of many mis-hits, in particular hitting behind the ball. The prime causes are too much use of the right hand from the top, and loss of tempo.

Some top pros have been known to suffer with this problem when playing pressure shots during the last few holes of an important championship. An apparently simple iron shot to the green results in an inexplicable miss. Pros often feel the loss of line happening, and their trained hands will eliminate a *complete* disaster, whereas the weekender's shot will be irretrievably doomed!

So it is in your own interests to try to eliminate this destructive fault.

*The answer lies in developing left side control and tempo.* Lessons 28 and 69 will help in this respect.

Many sportsmen who have excelled at sports such as cricket, tennis, badminton and squash are puzzled by their lack of progress at golf. They have been proud of their abilities as natural ball players and of the success they have achieved, but are frustrated by the apparently 'easy' game of golf.

The reason is that golf is primarily a left-handed game, ie, the left hand and side do all the leading. Therefore, sportspeople used to winning their matches by virtue of the strength in their right arm and wrist, find themselves unable to get results when they try the 'easy' game of golf!

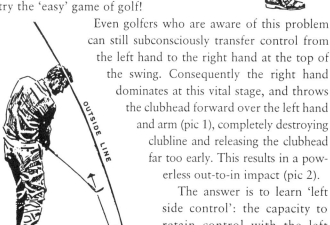

Even golfers who are aware of this problem can still subconsciously transfer control from the left hand to the right hand at the top of the swing. Consequently the right hand dominates at this vital stage, and throws the clubhead forward over the left hand and arm (pic 1), completely destroying clubline and releasing the clubhead far too early. This results in a powerless out-to-in impact (pic 2).

The answer is to learn 'left side control': the capacity to retain control with the left hand and arm. This is dealt with in lesson 28.

I estimate that during the time that it takes you to read this line, the phrases 'Head up' or 'Keep your head down' will have been uttered at least a thousand times somewhere throughout the golfing fraternity! This is because many golfers seem to think that lifting the head is the *cause* of a bad shot. Actually it is the PRODUCT of a bad swing!

This is mostly caused by massive stiffness at address and a paranoiac desire to keep the head down at all costs! Then when the swing does get underway, the only things that can move are the shoulders and head! So in this case the cause of 'Head up' was actually 'Head *down*!'

The PGA Training School wisely outlaws the instruction for the pupil to keep his head down at address. But 'Head down' is still the only rule for self-taught golfers.

If you want to make progress with your golf, the answer is to adopt a tension-free posture at address and to learn to swing the arms freely. Picture 1 will then be the result.

However, there is another reason for 'Head up'. That is when the player hits early, as in picture 2. Here, the player thinks he has already hit the ball, and then looks up! He will either hit the ground or play a weak shot. In good, free-swinging golfers, the player will *hit* 'late', and therefore *look* late!

Let's face it, most weekend golfers move the ball in the air in the direction they least want it to go – with a slice! But there are times when you actually want to manufacture a deliberate slice – or a 'fade', which is the hygienic name for a controlled slice!

The formula is easy to remember:

Simply line your whole body to the left of the flag, but keep the clubface square to the target – ie, aiming where you want the ball to finish (the clubface will appear 'open' as you look at it). When you swing, allow the clubhead to follow the line of your *body*, making sure that you do not turn the clubhead shut as you go through. This technique will produce the classic left-to-right flight on the ball.

It is worth adding that it is far easier to put side spin on a straight-faced club, ie, a No 4 or No 3 iron, than it is on a short iron. That is why a straight-faced driver will slice the ball much more viciously than a No 3 wood.

If you are already a slicer then the last thing you should do is practice this lesson!

There are times when you will need to move the ball from right to left. This has always been a most difficult shot for the handicap golfer to perform, particularly if he is plagued with a slice! However, we'll assume that you have that part under reasonable control.

Set yourself in a 'closed' address position as shown in the illustration. That is, with your entire body aiming to the right of the target but with the face of the club pointing straight down the target line.

When you swing, try to make the club follow the line of your shoulders. Make no attempt to manipulate the clubface in any way. This effectively reduces the loft of the club (it is far easier to hook using short irons through the fairway or a No 5 or No 3 wood off the tee).

As a point of interest, many weekend golfers actually stand 'closed' without realising it, but do not hook the ball. This is because they turn their shoulders towards the target on the downswing, which to them is hitting the ball 'straight'! Unfortunately, this procedure usually destroys the development of a good consistent swing.

There are many instances when the ability to hit a high or a low shot can save par or, better still, make a birdie.

The high shot: Play the ball off the inside of your left heel from a slightly open stance. Keep the hands level with the clubhead, not slightly ahead as you would when playing a normal pitch. If you wish to increase the loft you may open the clubface a little, as in a bunker shot. Play your usual swing and watch the result so that you will know what to expect when on the course.

The low shot: Play the ball back in your stance, just behind centre. This will ensure that your hands are well ahead of the ball. Keep your weight towards your left side. Keep hand action to a minimum and try to reproduce this position through impact.

Note: The high shot will tend to fade the ball to the right, so take an extra club – say a No 5 instead of a No 6 – to make the distance.

The low shot may well draw the ball to the left and run further than expected, so make allowances for this when planning your shots.

The general rule for these shots is to angle your body to match the slope without destroying your balance, and to make allowances with your club selection.

Uphill: Set your feet with more weight on your right leg and regard this as a prop. Try also to align your shoulders to the slope. When you make your backswing, avoid transferring more weight onto your right foot. On the downswing lean into the hill and try to keep the clubhead moving up the slope. Uphill shots add loft to your shots so take more club – say a five iron instead of a seven.

Downhill: Keep your right leg flexed more than your left, keep your weight held over this leg and try to keep it there as you make your backswing. On your throughswing, let your right side and the clubhead follow the contour of the slope. Downhill shots 'de-loft' your club so take, say, a seven iron instead of a five. Always bear in mind that these alterations should vary according to the severity of the gradients and conditions.

With side-hill lies, the simple rule is that the ball will follow the contour of the slope.

Feet below the ball: Choke down on the grip and swing the club on a flatter plane, like a baseball bat. The degree of 'flatness' will depend on the severity of the slope. Try to keep well balanced by leaning into the slope at address, and allow for the ball to move from right to left in flight. Limit the use of your body. Swing mainly with the hands and arms – not forgetting to make a shoulder turn on the backswing!

Feet above the ball: In this case your swing plane must be steeper to enable sufficient blade to connect with the ball. This leads to an unavoidable left-to-right flight, and this should be allowed for with your aiming. Do not try to hit the ball too hard as this will only lead to a total mis-hit.

Beginners find great difficulty in playing from awkward lies and should not feel disheartened if at first results are disappointing. Accurate striking requires a settled and technically correct swing. This of course takes time, practice, and a few lessons to achieve!

Note: The arrows indicate the line the ball should take and you should visualise this before you play.

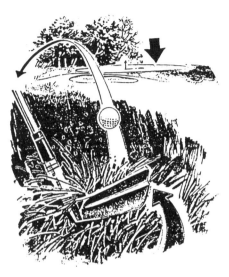

When your ball ends up in the rough the best thing to do is to accept your fate, and not expect to execute a miracle recovery shot!

One major problem is that the long grass will affect the type of control you have over the blade of the club because, as it approaches the ball, some grass will wrap round the hosel of your iron, forcing it to turn over, ie, shut or twist the toe inwards. This will send the ball to the left of the target.

The amount of backspin you can expect will also be limited, because of the effect of the grass that will get between the clubface and the ball.

So you should allow for both these factors when lining up and assessing your shot. In other words, aim right of the pin and expect a bit of a 'flyer'.

On the technical side: position the ball back in your stance. Using a well-lofted club, pick it up steeply on the backswing and hit down sharply, trying to make as clean a contact with the back of the ball as possible.

The chipping stroke could be compared in application to a long putting stroke. There is minimum wrist action used throughout.

Select a short iron, say a No 8 iron or a wedge, and set up with your feet quite close together, with the ball in the middle of your stance. Your shoulders should be square to the target line but your feet, legs and hips should face slightly left of target, ie, an 'open' stance.* Keep the hands slightly ahead of the ball throughout the shot.

The technique is to swing hands and arms back a short distance and sweep the ball off the turf with a slight descending blow, keeping the left wrist firm at impact and beyond. Keep the stroke short, crisp and rhythmical. This will produce sufficient backspin to give the shot control.

*Above all, never attempt to flick the ball into the air.*

Practice with various irons to get used to the response and the amount of roll on the ball. If you wish to keep it simple, concentrate on mastering one club – for instance, a pitching wedge. Many top players have great success with that method.

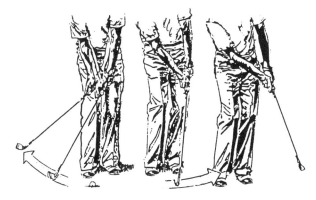

* Open and closed stances are explained in lesson 42.

Snooker is just as much a precision game as golf, particularly when it comes to putting.

Have you ever noticed a similarity between master putters on the professional golf tour, and the cueing action of world-class snooker players, such as Steve Davis or Stephen Hendry? There is one particular part of their cueing action which is well worth copying. You will notice that after a great snooker player has delivered his stroke he will hold his cue still and on line for a few seconds, usually until the ball is pocketed.

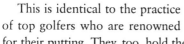

This is identical to the practice of top golfers who are renowned for their putting. They, too, hold the putter blade motionless after they have struck the ball. Some even wait for the 'death rattle' – the sound of the ball dropping into the hole – before moving. So why not try it out this week? It doesn't take a lot of practice and it has the additional benefit of making your putting stroke more positive.

Putting is a very serious business indeed, and it is also quite definitely 'a game within a game'.

The putting stroke itself usually has basic uniform features, such as smoothness and absolute steadiness of the body. However, putting grips are as individual as the person adopting them. Here, for the record, excluding the broom-handle method, are the most popular basic grips:

No 1 is used by Seve Ballesteros. Both forefingers are extended on either side of the shaft and the thumbs positioned on top. It has a reputation for 'feel' (until you miss one!).

No 2 is the standard reverse overlap (index finger over left hand) grip, which ensures that both hands work together and that the wrists stay firm.

No 3, with the left hand below the right, was devised to help golfers who suffered from the dreaded 'yips'. It keeps the left arm in control, and really does help!

No 4 is a further extension of the previous grip and is designed to take all hand action out of the putting stroke. This is Bernhard Langer's famous method for short putts, and he transformed his fortunes with it. It is as solid as a rock.

So take your pick – if none of the above work for you, invent your own!

When, for no accountable reason, you begin to miss easy putts it eats into your confidence. As a consequence your putting stroke becomes less positive.

When this happens, it is because the putter blade has decelerated as it approaches the ball, causing either a putt that is short or one that dribbles off line as it nears the hole. If this is your problem, then there is one exercise above all that could help you to regain your form.

Try this special acceleration drill:

Arrange a row of golf balls on the putting green. Place the putter head behind each ball and, without a backswing, roll the ball towards the target.

Practice until your action becomes smooth (with no double hits) and the ball rolls accurately on a straight line. Then try the same action using a very short backswing, no more than two or three inches (a peg behind the ball will help), remembering that the key is to always *accelerate* the putter head through the ball towards the cup.

Retain your positive attitude on course even if it means having to hole a few four-foot return putts!

Even in major championships you will witness top-class golfers failing to hole a short putt that could have secured them a victory. The same thing happens at club level – it is often the missed 'tiddler' that costs you the monthly medal!

So make for the practice green and try this highly effective putting drill:

Set up a selection of balls three to four feet from the hole and try to sink them all in succession, then increase the distance.

The object of the exercise is to move around the 'clock face', holing the balls in rotation. If you miss one, then you must go back and start all over again and keep repeating this until you have holed all the balls.

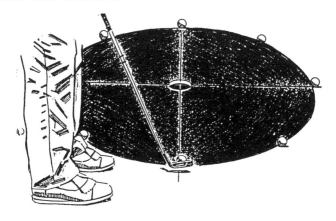

You may think that this is a fairly simple exercise, but you'd be surprised how often you will miss the last putt. In which case you must start all over again! This exercise enables you to get used to the build-up of pressure, and to treat the last ball as just another putt. Hopefully, when you next have a putt for the match, you will go into automatic and just slot it in!

When Eamon Darcy was asked to write an article on bunker play, this talented Irish golfer, with a swing peculiar to himself, refused. He thought it was all too simple.

'All you do,' he said, 'is open the blade, and give it a bit of a dig!'

When you come to think about it that's not a bad idea, because with bunker play you have more margin for error than any other golf shot. The technique is quite simple:

When you step into the sand, take your stance with the blade of your sand-iron facing the flag, then turn your whole body a few degrees to the left of target. Hold the clubhead above the ball – to touch the sand at address or on the backswing will incur a one-stroke penalty.

Remember to waggle your shoes into the sand to get a firm foothold, then aim at a point about two inches behind the ball and make your swing, following the path of your shoulder line. Imagine that you are going to slice a shallow divot under the ball from outside to in, and continue through to a full finish.

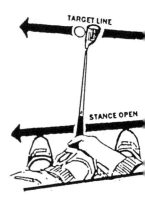

If you want to get more distance or height on the shot, then lay the blade open wider, take less sand, and, as Eamon would say: 'Give it an *extra* little dig!'

A good tempo enables you to perform the swing action that you have learned, no matter what the conditions. It is a conditioning process that supplants your reflex – that involuntary instinct to develop power before it is required, ie, hitting early.

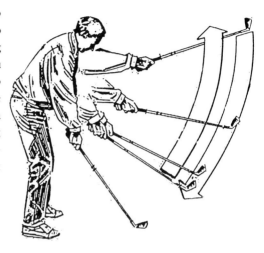

Tempo does not mean swinging slower (slower than what?). It is overall smoothness, which is signified by apparent lack of effort. Such players as Fred Couples and Ernie Els display this feature admirably. Tempo should only be worked on when all technical problems have been resolved. It is the final touch that allows a player to retain his form.

'But, how can I visualise smoothness?' you might well ask. Well, here is a very special exercise to help you gain good tempo:

Take your address position, with your arms hanging free, then swing the club up in front of you *very, very slowly*. Lower the club down again to the ball. Repeat this action several times without hurrying, while retaining your exact address position. This will give you a visual and physical image that you can copy when you take your swing.

This is a cumulative exercise that will, with constant repetition, develop a smooth, professional tempo.

A shank (or socket) is the most destructive shot in golf! It occurs when the ball connects with the blade just where the hosel, or shank, joins the shaft. The effect is to make the ball shoot off at an acute angle to the right (pic 1).

At worst, it can cause a succession of similar shots, particularly with a wedge. But what can a player do if this happens when he is mid-round?

The nearest thing to an instant cure was demonstrated to me some years ago by the late, renowned golf instructor Leslie King, and I have seen it work so many times that I am prepared to guarantee its success!

First, you must accept that you are striking the ball on the shank – and do not question why! Now deliberately address the ball on that part of the club, ie, the shank, then take the clubhead back about twelve inches and return it, once again *on the shank* (pic 2). Repeat this procedure twice more. Then immediately make your usual full backswing and concentrate on striking the

ball on the exact *middle* of the clubface. As if by a miracle, this will happen and your shank will be cured!

So, if ever the 'unmentionables' happen to you on course, don't despair – try the miracle cure!

I am frequently asked to advise an older player whose handicap has risen from a respectable twelve to well over twenty. One swing is enough to tell me that his 'method' has not stood the test of time. Invariably his set-up will be tight and rigid, and his backswing short and wristy.

In youth, when the body is lithe and supple, a player can get away with these technically unorthodox methods. But if no attempt is made to keep the body flexible, then the golf swing will simply grind to a halt.

There is no gimmick to retrieve this situation; the only real answer is to restyle your swing. Gary Player was forced to do just that, but his new method of going 'walkies' after impact is really too extreme!

The answer is to start on a programme of gradually freeing up your arms and gently encouraging your hips and torso to turn adequately. Lessons 12, 24 and 72 will help. Many elder statesmen have benefited from these recommendations and exercises.

From this the message should be clear: choose your method of play carefully. By all means lock your arms onto your chest and use your body for power; but if you do, you'll be living on borrowed time!

Alternatively, join the free swingers and have yourself a swing for life! Hale Irwin is a fine example of this.

## **Lesson 72** The Swing Shape Exercise

This exercise was devised by the legendary golf instructor Leslie King. Without doubt, he left a wonderful legacy to help golfers to learn and maintain their swings. It is the entire swing action in a single exercise, and you don't even need a club to do it!

However, it must be learned to perfection, preferably with the aid of a mirror. You really must try to master it, otherwise you cannot expect your swing to fall into place when you hold a golf club.

*1. Adopt the correct address position, ensuring that your left shoulder is naturally higher than your right, then grasp your left wrist with your right hand.*

*2. Now perform your backswing by swinging your left hand and arm up to the top as described in my lessons. Be sure that, as you swing your arm up, your weight remains 'down'. This will ensure maximum upper arm leverage.*

*(This part of the exercise helps you to sense that the body turns to permit a free swing of the left hand and arm. You will also sense the need to raise the left heel slightly in order to achieve full left arm leverage).*

*3. By making a free downward swing of your left arm and correct foot action you will arrive back at your address position with your shoulders square, and the back of your left hand at the target. Any other downswing formula will render this academic position an impossibility.*

4. *Once you have mastered your left-arm downswing technique it is time to let your arms swing through to a balanced finish. Notice that there is no gratuitous back-bending, or flailing arms, both of which are indicative of overuse of the body. Instead, the arms have swung through to a high-controlled finish, supported from the waist up by a straight back.*

As you perform this exercise you will realise that a responsive and perfectly balanced body enables the left arm to swing fully and freely. It also places the arms in the correct position at the top – automatically.

If you live with this exercise, your swing too will live happily ever after!

Picture 1: If you reach the top of your backswing in this position, then you are in company with world-class golfers! Here is your check: your left heel is raised with the pressure felt on the inside of that foot. This provides upward resistance to allow you momentarily to hold your shoulders in a fully-turned position. This 'upward resistance' powers the hands as they begin to swing down. Therefore the means of controlling your shoulders is established before the downswing begins.

Picture 2: As soon as the left hand and arm gets under way the left heel returns to the ground and 'lateral shift' commences. The body unwinds from the feet up, ie, feet, then legs, hips and lastly the shoulders. In a split-second the release of the club will begin, and the right leg will become active. This foot and leg activity creates the resistance that will enable the hands and wrists to retain power through impact. This lower body and leg activity takes place *really fast* in order to establish the resistance *before* impact takes place.

Picture 3: Impact! The right knee has begun to fold in towards the left. This creates the conditions for the transfer of resistance to the small of the back after impact. The hands and clubhead are in vertical alignment at the moment of impact. The shoulders are square to the intended line of flight. This ensures that the clubface will remain squarely on that line through impact, providing a sustained contact with the ball.

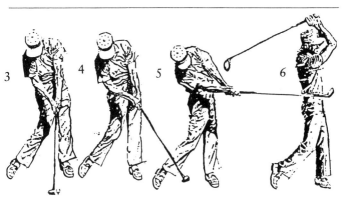

Pictures 4 and 5: Important! The wrists do not roll through or after impact. The hands, wrists and arms are in exactly the same relationship as they were at address. When the shoulders turn after impact this relationship remains unchanged. If the blade is closed or rolled at or after impact, it is only a matter of time before it happens *prior* to impact. This is how wild hooks are born!

After impact, as the arms pass the body, the resistance passes to the small of the back, which 'moves in' in the direction of the target to set up a counter-force to the swing of the hands and arms. In so doing, the 'hip turn' occurs to allow the arms to swing freely up into the finish.

Picture 6: The correct foot and leg action has created a position of perfect balance, which is held from the waist up. The hands have free-wheeled to a high finish and there is clear evidence that power has been delivered along a line.

If you get all of this in place, you can give up your day job and turn pro! It is my sincere hope that these lessons will inspire you to try to attain a high standard of golf, free from frustration.

(The author is indebted to the late Leslie King for this analysis of the true golf swing.)

*Happy golfing!*
*Bill Brampton, The Swing Doctor*

A good swing can be spoiled by bad practice!
Driving ranges provide excellent practice
facilities, but if you are an ambitious golfer
here is a note of caution:

Do not purchase large quantities of balls
and fire them off in
machine-gun fashion
in an attempt to
'groove your swing'
because, without
realising it, your swing will
get quicker and quicker, with
destructive results.

Keep your swing smooth and
unhurried at all times and relax for a full
minute after six or seven shots. Study a
top tournament player's routine – he will
commence with a few short pitches and
gradually work up to the longer irons. He
will also take plenty of time between each
shot. So copy the pros who know!

Work to maintain your swing shape
and delivery, and seek a relaxed, balanced finish, from which you can check
the position of your clubface (pic 1).

If you find that you are playing your long irons or driver
poorly, do not persist with this club. Discard it temporarily, turn
instead to a mid-iron and work at delivering the clubhead
squarely to the back of the ball (pic 2). Then try again with the
club that was giving you difficulty.

Above all, never work only with your driver, or simply try for as much distance as possible. Exhaustion and frustration will be the certain end result. Far better to choose a middle-distance target and aim to group your shots as accurately as possible.

Avoid swivelling the mat or altering your stance against the natural lines of the mat. It can lead to optical confusion and affect the shape of your swing.

Finally, at the first signs of tiredness or boredom – stop! Although the temptation will be great to 'get this thing right', further practice will only do harm, so I say again – *stop!* Little and often is far better than an infrequent assault on a big basket of balls!

Remember, knowing how to practice, and doing lots of it, can seriously improve your golf!

'Quick fixes' (and 'fixes') do a disservice to golfers by promising a short-term benefit at the expense of long-term damage!

By experimenting with a 'fix' a golfer can totally disrupt a reasonable action. Because of the complexity of the golf swing no amateur can accurately self-diagnose his own swing problems – that is a fact. To apply the wrong 'fix' to a fault can have disastrous and lasting ill effects. 'Fixes' (it sounds more potent than 'tip', but is the same thing!) are the latest fashion, peddled for their eye-catching appeal. My advice: close your eyes to them, and simply return to checking and relying on sound fundamentals, preferably under the eyes of a qualified tutor.

## Swing Aids and Gimmicks

I believe that there is no mechanical device or passive swing aid that can replace the proper process of structured learning from a competent instructor. Neither do I accept that a teacher should be applauded for wedging a beach-ball between a player's legs or strapping him into a harness or such-like. Surely, if the teacher's analysis of the golf swing is one hundred percent sound, then no such gimmickry should ever be required to make it work. Let me explain:

Great swingers from the past and of the present rely on an armoury of 'muscle memory feels' (which they developed from constant practice) in their hands and body to call on in case of emergency. Contrast this with the gimmick-reliant player who cannot 'get it back' until he is once again locked into a contraption or immersed in the 'wonders' of the latest 'brilliant' gimmick or 'magic move'!

## 'Amateur Pros'

Golf is a difficult enough game without the pleasure-golfer meddling in a subject that requires years of specialist training, and sometimes a lifetime of experience, to understand. No amateur, no matter how accomplished, should ever think he knows enough to fix his own swing, let alone set about giving advice to a friend or partner – typically 'Keep your head down!' I once heard of a player who said to his partner: 'I don't know anything about the golf swing, but I know what you are doing wrong!' That is not the end of the story – his partner listened!

Avoid the temptation to give advice, and take it only from the people qualified to give it – The Professionals!